island living

island living

Inland Retreats and Shoreside Havens

Linda Leigh Paul

UNIVERSE

First published in the United States of America in 2005
by UNIVERSE PUBLISHING
A Division of Rizzoli International Publications, Inc.
300 Park Avenue South
New York, NY 10010
www.rizzoliusa.com

2005 2006 2007/ 10 9 8 7 6 5 4 3 2 1

Designed by Lynne Yeamans/Lync

Printed in China

ISBN: 0-7893-1306-5

Library of Congress Catalog Control Number: 2005927424

PAGE 4: *An aeriel view of Anacapa Island at sunset.*
© *George H. H. Huey/CORBIS*
PAGE 10: *The windblown sand covering a seashell.*
© *George H. H. Huey/CORBIS*
PAGE 12: *A ghost crab on the beach.*
© *George H. H. Huey/CORBIS*
PAGE 14: *The detail of a butterfly wing.*
© *Ralph A. Clevenger/CORBIS*
PAGE 15: *A close-up of a monarch butterfly egg.*
© *George D. Lepp/CORBIS*
PAGE 16: *A detail of scarlet macaw feathers.*
© *Stuart Westmorland/CORBIS*
PAGE 18: *The mist at the shore of Mount Desert Island.*
© *Owaki - Kulla/CORBIS*

acknowledgments

Intrigue preserves our love affairs with islands. Ancient and living geology, neoteric opinions about the speed of evolution, cultural prophecies, and sensory perceptions are the essence of island life. And still, time spent on an island is a journey to the center of a specific and small compass. A stay is an experience that begins on identifiable ground and presses into consuming trails of light and shadow, fringes and vignettes, where cricket-green leaves clutch vines among wet falls and trickling streams. It is the sort of place where a slow row of turquoise diamonds crosses a sunny path and slinks into an outer dark edge. Where the triangular shapes turn white—on the back of a snake. Where we are suddenly struck by the similarities of bright white light, green foliage, turquoise camouflage, and an unforeseen comprehension of the color of a robin's eggs. Philosopher Ludwig Wittgenstein wrote in the *Tractatus*: "whereof one cannot speak, thereof one must remain silent." He means, I think, that the center of the compass is exactly where you are and what you alone comprehend, and often, it is a place that we know to be far too extraordinary to describe.

My appreciation to the island residents for their graciousness and participation is immeasurable. Many shared their treasures, along with their views on land and resource conservation and preservation. Many have expressed their reverence for the earth, as well as their efforts for its improved future. For architects, my respect and admiration grows with each new project. I owe a debt of gratitude to Peter Forbes, F.A.I.A., for his bold and delicate designs; David Coleman for a breathtaking and masterful project; John and Cornelia Brewer for introducing us to Bequia and Moonhole. To John DiMaio for resourcefulness and wonderful images. I would like to express my love and gratitude to Dawna Miller for her unwavering support during the last year and a half. And to all who formed the circle of friends: Richard Galarneau, whose wit and love of life and laughter is nonpareil; poet Geraldine Helen Foote, the source of many, if not all, things; Marilyn Booth Love, for her unlimited grace and strength; Janet and Stuart Jones for their guidance, knowledge, and patience; Junie Cleaver, Elisabeth Jung, and everyone's best friend, Kerry Hampton. A special thank you to Michael and Petra and Megan Mathers.

I am particularly grateful, in this past year and always, for the opportunity to work with editor extraordinaire, Alex Tart. Ever present, yet elusive, Alex balanced an armful of twins, James and Andrew, while guiding this project to its happy conclusion. I am especially grateful for this project and to Rizzoli's very generous publisher, Charles Miers, for every opportunity he has given me to work with Universe.

And to Robert Paul, the master of the universe(s), my own, especially, who knows what it meant and also, what it means.

CONTENTS

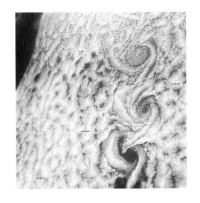

PART I: Capturing the Horizon

PART II: Into the Bold

introduction

"Coffee and oranges in a sunny chair,
And the green freedom of a cockatoo" [1]

Island life is a dream of abundance, well-being, and perfumed air, an enchantment of orchestral bird songs in the twilight. Butterfly wings fan horizons into a shimmer in the cool of the dawn, and a wash of soft, bubble-fronted waves meets the day's first imprints in the sand. Every island is a vision of an Edenic beach that sparkles with gems and eccentric vegetation, ripe with fruit that never falls. They are the homes of the gods and the Great Mothers of myth, the Blessed and the sprites. There we can yield to our impulses to be barefoot, get wet. And they, the islands, are the source of our exotic, undying wonder. They are the source of Henri Bergson's *élan vital*, the intuitively perceived and mysterious life force.

How did such dreams of heaven on earth emerge after centuries of the darker, fantastic tales about the nature of islands and what took place on them, stories of heathen lands where helpless souls awaited judgment or worse? Landing on an uninhabited island meant a life too far beyond the reach of civilization to be saved, a perpetual *New Yorker* cartoon of an unshaven man leaning against a lone palm tree. For a shipwrecked scattering of humanity washed up on a pebbled island shore, there could be only despair, loneliness, hardship, and death.

Islands were home to the destitute, the diseased, the shanghaied, and the convicted. Surrounded by the cruel sea that took them there, and the horizon, in places unmarked on navigational charts, the castaways were in a prison and a struggle for survival: not a measure of time in paradise.

The horrible myths and dread of the old tales slowly faded when a restorative adventure began to work its way to the lore of the seafarers. One such story of salvation and redemption in an island setting tells of the shipwreck of the British ship *Sea Venture*, in 1609. Its voyage to the new world ended when the ship was caught up in a storm and dashed onto the rocks near an island. All hands washed up on what was believed to be the most forlorn group of islands on earth, commonly called the Devil's Islands. They were the known homes of devils and wicked spirits. They were, in fact, the Bermudas. Navigators feared and avoided them above all others, as they would have avoided the twin pulls of *Scylla* (the monster) and *Charybdis* (the whirlpool), the two tempestuous forces described in *The Odyssey* who faced each other in a narrow strait. After the loss of their vessel, the *Sea Venture*'s survivors salvaged iron, wood, and rigging from the battered ship and from them built a smaller one. The broken spirits of the shipwrecked crew were revived by a miracle of deliverance. They left the island after nine months of rebuilding—refreshed, comforted, and confident—to ferry themselves to their original destination, Virginia. Afterward, the ship's Captain Newport ("and Divers Others") wrote that despite their initial fear of a place the Devil himself would shun, they found the air sweet and the island full of all the necessities for the preservation and enjoyment of life: "it [was] in truth, the richest, healthfulest, and pleasing and . . . utterly natural land as ever man set foot upon." [2] Among testimonies from the survivors was a letter by one of the ship's officers, William Strachey. He wanted the Bermudas revelations to be known, and with them, the knowledge that comes with experience. He wrote: "Truth is the daughter of Time, and men ought not to deny everything which is not subject to their own sense." [3]

An impression on our souls, made by reality itself, gives us an unshakable grasp of some part of this reality, which could not possibly have come from something that is not real. Shakespeare found enough veracity in the miracle of the *Sea Venture* to use it as the setting—in a visionary realm—for *The Tempest*.

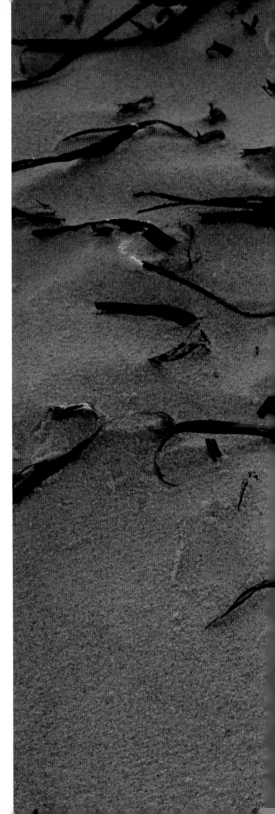

Truth, time, and experience. These are the mysteries that begin to unravel as we learn to slow down, take a closer look, and listen to the sounds of Nature. "Island time" channels our observations into a physical immediacy. A friend, when she was a small girl, was often drawn to the uneven lift and fall of a butterfly's wings. She was charmed, watched quietly and closely, and felt she could have spent two years or the whole of eternity watching the movements and sensing the raw silk feel of those gloriously colored wings. Their design seemed dyed in *ikat* fashion, a network of reticular forms, reminiscent of the rare pattern on the hide of the Kenyan giraffe. She discovered, much later, that in contemplating those lines on that wing, on that day, her emotional composure allowed her to experience the boundaries of time. *She* decided when time existed and where it was absent. Her soul was impressed with an unmistakable grasp of the butterfly, a reality called a *cataleptic* impression: It is not simply a route to knowledge, it *is* knowledge.

We once believed that the earth was very large, and we, the creatures of it, were very small, and our knowledge of the world was very difficult to grasp. Now, our pace has accelerated, the earth has become small, and we are large: We

must always be thinking and there is never enough time. We can cause time to slow or even to disappear if we quell the impulse to always be thinking. We can reengage ourselves within our surroundings if we take a slower, closer look at them, and dwell in the soothing ancestral realm of our senses. Our inner light may sometimes shine on the distant

habits of civilization, yet finally flicker out. We may see that it isn't really *all* of civilization that we want; and . . . we do not have to have what we do not want. To realize that life is what we *are* at any second will force the moment to its crisis. We can be inspired to design and build, to write music, to paint, by what we look at and our way of looking at it.

A butterfly's egg can inspire a scientist, an architect, or a sculptor. The complex beauty of its luminescence; the narrow, slender flutes and the long rows of tiny French-button shapes; the egg set securely in microscopic, crinolated, crystalline fibers, is a model for space stations, *haute couture*, or ingenious architecture. The approach of a flock of scarlet

ibis, signaled by the hastening sound of thousands of individual wings heard a mile away, alerts us that something rare and strange is about to happen: A crescendo, a landing, and the lightning of cymbals! can teach us to listen to the winds, the waves, and ourselves. Perhaps the ability to recognize individual birds or turtles, the sound of ibis or bees, is the same skill as running fleet-footed through a forest on no marked path, letting "your feet think for themselves, deciding where to land, what to go around, what to go over and under . . . the best route simply presents itself, without having to be thought out,"[4] and you realize the intrinsic truth of the impression on your soul that was made by running freely. Running freely, calming the impulse to always be thinking, considering most carefully the world at your feet—these may be ways of getting to an island.

"He's being sent to an island. That is to say, he is being sent to a place where he'll meet the most interesting set of men and women to be found anywhere in the world. All the people, who, for one reason or another, have got too self-consciously individual to fit into community life. All the people who aren't satisfied with orthodoxy, who've got independent ideas of their own. Every one, in a word, who's any one." [5]

The owners of the houses presented in this book might be those very same ones who no longer wish to shine their internal lights on the orthodoxies of twenty-first-century life. No island is an island any longer, but I wonder, how could we ever have dared to think of disturbing this beautiful universe?

notes

1 Wallace Stevens, *Sunday Morning, Harmonium* (New York: Alfred A. Knopf, 1923), pp. 100-04.

2 Sir Thomas Gates, Sir George Miers and Captain Newport, *A Discovery of the Barmudas, Otherwise Called the Isle of Devils* (London: John Windet, 1610).

3 William Strachey, *A True Repertory of the Wreck and Redemption of Sir Thomas Gates, Knight, upon and from the Islands of the Bermudas, et.al.,* (In Samuel Purchas, *Purchas His Pilgrims*: 1625) Part 4, Book 9, Chapter 6, pp. 1734 ff.

4 *Shelter* (California: Shelter Publications, 1973), p. 95.

5 Aldous Huxley, *Brave New World* (New York: HarperCollins, 1998), p. 227.

PART I capturing the horizon

A steep welcoming quiet at the front door.

haiku

OWNERS: William S. and Paula Merwin
DESIGNER: William S. Merwin
PHOTOGRAPHER: John DiMaio

William Merwin designed the Haiku house to be constructed deep within the palms and trees, so visitors wouldn't see it until they were almost upon it. An urban eye might view it as a kind of long tree house: one end is twenty feet high up in the trees, the other is anchored to a slope. The tree-covered portion was William's design as a natural ventilation system to keep cool and refreshing air circulating within the house in the midst of the tropical heat and sunlight. The design is so thoroughly adapted to the movements of its inhabitants (and vice-versa) that their work, meditation, dining, and leisure habits express a vigorous harmony with the generative influences of every well-used room.

To reach the front door, one travels down an abundantly planted stone path. There, greeted by a pair of beautifully glazed Foo dogs, is the lanai, which William claims "is permanently cluttered with garden tools." William and his wife, Paula, are a presence in their land. The deforested, barren, and eroded land they first encountered on the promontory of the nearby ridge bore little more than parched grass and scrub guava. William later learned that the whole coast had once been a forest. But on that first day, downslope from the bleak ridge, he came to another island world: "the dark green cloud of the mango trees, under them, in the shade . . . was the shadowy stream bed with its rocks under the huge trees that made me want to stay and so to settle, and have a garden in this valley." [1]

A garden, of course, is by design, but the "illusion of a forest" can be accomplished by human effort. William wanted to restore

ABOVE: *A pathside altar in honor of the earth and its governing spirits.* OPPOSITE: *The path leads through palms to a guest house.*

or repair the abused land. His goal was to plant native species and try to bring the landscape back to what it might have looked like if it had been left undisturbed. Their permanent collection of garden tools has assisted William and Paula's drive to plant more than three hundred species of palm trees, some of them highly endangered. All the plants on the property are individual cultivations, many from seed. The ancient argument between the philosophers and the poets about the nature of human life and how to live it becomes irrelevant in a world where nature is forever altered. Every mindful effort is one that will bring the garden back to us. William writes for us to learn: "There are young trees in the ground. The days are much too short, they go by too fast, and we wish for rain and the sound of water among the rocks."[2]

1. Jane Garmey, ed., *The Writer in the Garden*, Algonquin Books (Chapel Hill, 1999), p. 15.
2. *Ibid*, p. 19.

OPPOSITE: *A window through an island jungle to a waterfall.* ABOVE: *A lanai designed and built for the enjoyment of cool morning and mid-day fare.*

ABOVE: *The dining area is warmed by the wood of the harvest table and wood floors. The silver frogs holding candles glow.*
BELOW: *The dojo, Zen meditation (zazen) room has been used since before the rest of the house was finished.* OPPOSITE: *The living room with an elegant, relaxed feel, just opposite the dining area in the large central room.*

ABOVE: *A corner collection of miniature sea turtles, precious mementos, and treasures.* BELOW: *Paula's study exerts its own aliveness and joy.* OPPOSITE: *The walls of William and Paula's library speak, to us.*

The overall house is two simple shed-roof structures joined by a raised deck and walkway.

vinalhaven

OWNERS: Charles Lowrey and Susan Rodriguez
ARCHITECT: Susan T. Rodriguez, FAIA
PHOTOGRAPHER: Jeff Goldberg / ESTO

Susan's house is located on a small private island in the Penobscot Bay, about twelve miles off the coast of Maine. The design emerged as a natural outcome of the limits and opportunities prompted by the remote location and the fragility of the landscape. The owners also wanted to be engaged with the island's working waterfront. Spectacular summer sunsets and scenes of boat traffic helped determine room height and orientation. Also contributing to the design process was the need to capture rainwater, a desire for easy maintenance, a short building season, and

the guidelines of a Maine Coast Heritage Trust review.

The cabin sits on a bluff overlooking a narrow nautical passage into which the summer sun aligns. The building form is composed of two simple shed-roof structures, joined by a raised deck and a walkway. The two pitched roof structures are an essential part of the water collection system on the island. The larger of the two buildings opens to the ocean views, while the smaller cabin faces the wooded island landscape. A grand stair between the two provides access to a sloped field to the west. This ensemble is almost

hidden in the landscape from the water, yet allows dramatic views from within.

The detailing of the cabin is meant to animate the simple forms with shade and shadow, highlighting many of the functional aspects of the design. These include the gutter and down spouts system, bracketed roof overhangs, and shutters.

The primary building material is wood. A repetitive, precut, post-and-beam hemlock structure was built on a wood frame base in two and a half days. The exterior is white cedar shingles. The interior follows the rational order of the

exterior building with exposed posts and beams. A continuous clerestory window in the larger cabin disengages the sloping roof plane from the vertical wall surface, allowing the structure to visually penetrate from interior to exterior. The larger cabin houses the main living space, with sleeping accommodations on two levels and storage below. The smaller cabin provides flexible space for sleeping or recreation and houses three water cisterns below.

Spending even brief periods of time twelve miles from the mainland requires considerable planning. The island has its own independent infrastructure. Propane powers the appliances and lighting, and a small generator is used for pumping water and septic. A water tower, set at the island's highest point, pressurizes the system. A wood stove provides heat, when necessary. As the natural weathering of the cedar shingles and pine decking takes place, over time the buildings will become further reconciled into their setting.

ABOVE: *The raised deck between the two buildings. In the rear the cabin faces into the island interior.* OPPOSITE: *The natural weathering of the wooden buildings will, over time, seamlessly blend the buildings into the setting.*

OPPOSITE: *The interior of exposed post and beam in the main living space reflects the outside character of the building.*

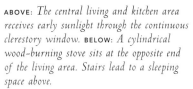

ABOVE: *The central living and kitchen area receives early sunlight through the continuous clerestory window.* BELOW: *A cylindrical wood-burning stove sits at the opposite end of the living area. Stairs lead to a sleeping space above.*

LEFT: *The kitchen offers easy access to exterior decks and walkways.* RIGHT: *Sunlight shining through the clerestory brightens tall spaces above the living room.* BELOW: *A spare and spacious bedroom is nearly nestled in the trees.*

Clingstone: built on the largest of the Dumpling Islands.

clingstone

OWNER: Henry A. Wood, FAIA, Kallmann McKinnell & Wood Architects, Inc.
BUILDER: J. D. Johnstone
PHOTOGRAPHER: John DiMaio

This striking silhouette, emerging from its rock, is Clingstone. It is located on the largest of the islands known, since the 1700s, as the Dumplings in the East Passage of Narragansett Bay, in Rhode Island. Two miles from the harbor in Newport, the house and its island are at the edge of the main passage from the open ocean to the bay.

The house was built as a summer cottage in 1904–05 by Joseph Lovering Wharton of Philadelphia (a distant cousin of Mr. Wood), after his own nearby house was taken by the government to build Fort Wetherill in anticipation of an attack on Newport during the Spanish-American War. It was

designed by J. D. Johnstone, with much guidance from luminist painter William Trost Richards and Wharton himself. Richards's former house had also been taken for the fort, and he first purchased this island as a "favor" for Wharton; Richards's initials are carved in a granite block in the stone wall to the southeast. Designed in the shingle style, with heavy timbers, the house is unusual in that its interior walls are also shingled. Each of its twenty-three rooms has a different tint. The shingles were thought to eliminate the cracking plaster seen in many nearby houses when the fort coast defense guns were first used.

Many utilities were installed in the house during the Wharton

period. Water was collected at the roof and funneled into a large cistern. Tubs had a choice of fresh or salt water for bathing; toilets were salt. Coal-fired steam heat was provided after a coal barge broke up on the rock and left its cargo behind. Electricity was installed in the 1920s, supplied by a diesel generator on the jetty.

The Wharton family summered in the house until 1941, and it lay vacant until Mr. Wood purchased it in 1961. By then, the house had suffered damage from vandalism, pigeons, and storms. It has been restored and preserved by the Wood family over the past forty-four years. The Woods' children spend most

A massive fireplace faces into three rooms: the living room (shown), a billiards room (on right), and the pantry and kitchen (to the left).

weekends at Clingstone from the beginning of May through the end of October each year. Their goal is to maintain and enjoy this one-hundred-year-old treasure.

Eventually ownership will pass from Henry A. Wood to his sons. The three brothers work at retrofitting the house for future self-containment and sustainability. Fresh water is still collected on the roof, but it is now treated and filtered. There is a solar hot water system. Saltwater is no longer an option in the tubs, however. The saltwater toilets are being replaced by composting systems. Plenty of electricity is now being produced by a 1,500-watt windmill and photovoltaic panels, which are capable of running everything. Both DC and AC electricity are used. Propane gas is brought from shore for cooking, as is an occasional supply of potable water. The house is elegantly reconnected to its origins and its original purpose: independence. All it needs now, claims son Josh Wood, is an electric boat.

OPPOSITE: *Built-in wood and glass cabinetry line the walls of the pantry and dining room.*

ABOVE: *A study and office for drafting and chart making.* LEFT: *The view from the master bedroom over the bay.*

The main entry hall and staircase. Exterior shingles used on interiors were believed to deter cracking in the plaster walls. The "sculpture" is the nose cone from a minuteman missile.

The Avalon house looks out over the inland waterway.

avalon

OWNER: Martha Wright
ARCHITECT: Robert A. Johnson, The Johnson Group
PHOTOGRAPHER: John DiMaio

The sounds heard from the red barn are orchestral and in concert with their surroundings. The scene: a panorama of the Cedar Island Bird Sanctuary and the inland waterway. This is nature, old form.

An individual with the quality of mind and a temperament that is almost instinctive—one who does not give up, doesn't alter direction, and always senses her destination—is, too, a creature of nature. Martha Wright knew where she wanted to live and built a plan, year after year, on finding a house on the water in Avalon, New Jersey, thirteen miles north of Cape May. She found a waterfront lot never touched by the hand of construction. When asked what environmental concerns she had about the area, Martha Wright acknowledged, "it's too late for that; it's been stripped, sanitized, and sterilized with pebble lawns, instant landscaping, and plastic houses."

The house that Martha built is efficiency stripped to its beautiful bones. She incorporated precautions into the design to prevent inadvertent and unwanted over-consumption: no closets, no air conditioning, no Sheetrock, no vinyl or aluminum. Her design process consisted of continuous refinement and reduction to quality, restored basics. For example, in her ingenious cupola design, Martha devised a system to draw the heat up and out of the place with a simple fan. Her decisions and specifications were carefully worked into drawings by architect Robert Johnson, the well-loved visionary of many waterfront cottages and homes. With Robert's guidance, the project transformed itself into splendid simplicity.

Pine interiors on the first floor and an open stair leading up to two bedrooms define a casual beach life. The bedroom level hosts beautifully whitewashed pine-clad interiors with French doors that open to views of the water, over the marsh, and into the sky. The upstairs balcony is a

LEFT: *A magic walk is down the wooden path, through the pampas grass and onto the boat ramp out to the water.* OPPOSITE: *The north side of the house is prepared for "weather." Sliding barn-board shutters cover the first and second floor doors and windows.*

platform for following the paths of egrets, osprey, and migrating flocks that count on the bird sanctuary from year to year.

Life on the water anywhere is subject to vicious weather, and the farm-red barn at Avalon is prepared. Flood tides and "northeasters" called for a twelve-foot elevation on pilings. The northern exposure is hung with sliding barn-board shutters that cover the first-floor French doors and a second-story window. (The same barn-board feature is used on the interior to tuck away the first-floor bathroom and give a soft brushed red barn color to the inside of the living area.)

In the midst of what could be viewed as an architecturally toxic site, Martha's barn stands for something and stands its ground. Her protection of the bird sanctuary and the waterways, evident in her courage to live off the consumer radar map, is her greatest reward.

LEFT: *The twelve-foot elevation of the house on piles gives a better view of the dock and waterway.* ABOVE: *The uniquely compact kitchen is complete with a vintage GE "monitor top" icebox and a 1940s Chambers range.*

The master bedroom shows off an iron "campaign" bed, which had been used during harvest migrations by French peasants.

*This glorious Gothic revival houses a
collection of modern joys and amenities.*

fishers island

ARCHITECTS: Mark Simon, FAIA, and Leonard J. Wyeth, AIA, Centerbrook Architects and Planners
PHOTOGRAPHER: Timothy Hursley / Arkansas Office

This house revels in its eccentricity, but with precedent: the Gothic revival of nearby houses; American craftsman idiosyncrasies; and the rambling, connected vernacular farm buildings of New England. The house is a fusion of old and new, packing the traditional with a collection of modern volumetric surprises and new spatial relationships. These and the constantly shifting light and views of the interiors and the landscape keep this house good humored, and provide endless entertainment to its many guests.

The home enjoys a high, windswept site on Fishers Island, which has views to the north, across the Long Island Sound to the Connecticut shoreline. Approached from the west, it appears as a tribe of connected buildings, a brood of structures surrounding a "mother house." They share a resemblance in their cedar shingle siding, dark gabled roofs, and the abstract stickwork. A porte cochere, created by the extension of the roof of the storage shed over the driveway, leads into a small gravel court where the main house faces a "drunken fence" to the south. The pickets here begin straight and then gradually stumble along. The house's gabled court face has windows that are also gabled, giving some order to their otherwise random placement.

There are six exterior doorways that are protected by roofed gates. Each gate has a variation of the stick design and sits next to the house in its own way. The meandering structures outside only hint at the colliding spaces inside. Here, within taut exterior walls, formally shaped rooms are placed in balanced chaos, shaken like toy blocks in a box. Cylindrical, elliptical, cubical, and rectangular spaces are

ABOVE: *Two of the six roofed gates that protect each of the exterior doorways.* RIGHT: *The long roofed gate at the main entrance nestles into the porte cochere to offer shelter to guests.*

comfortable, functional, familiar, and easy to live within. The groupings offer unexpected spatial changes when moving from one room to another and a new land-scape view at each doorway.

The circular entry hall leads to many directions. A crooked stair-case painted cornflower blue, next to the front door, lets in daylight

Seemingly lonely and unfrequented in the muffled fog, the house is in fact eccentric and light in the interior.

from above. Farther to the right, a tall hall descends to a tiny circular chamber, then into the rolling ellipse of the living room. This high-ceilinged space is countered with a cornice of stickwork several feet below the ceiling. The rectangular dining room is several steps above the living room. Snug in between the dining room and a square kitchen is a tiny library.

At the top of the stairs on the second floor is a circular antechamber leading to the oval master bedroom. Inside is a gabled alcove that pokes out of the house as the balcony gate, with views north to the Long Island Sound. The master bed imitates tree branches. The house blends the designs of nature and the forms of geometry for a lively yet comforting meditation in the landscape.

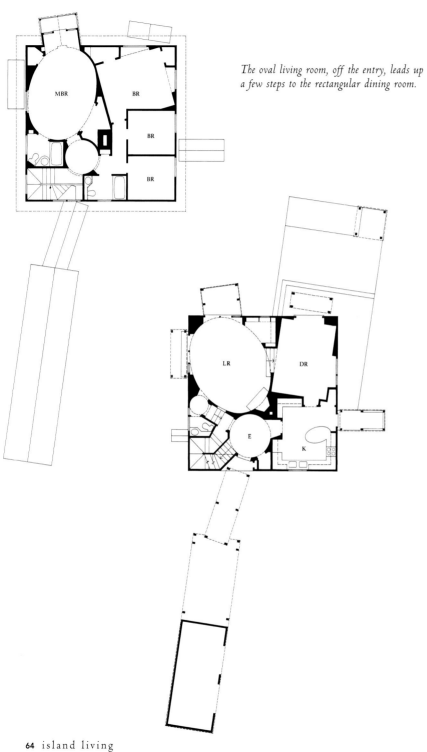

The oval living room, off the entry, leads up a few steps to the rectangular dining room.

MBR

BR

BR

BR

LR

DR

E

K

OPPOSITE: *The dining room opens to a view underneath the abstract stickwork of the roofed gate.* ABOVE: *A hand-carved headboard softly mimics the stickwork of the deck rail outside the oval-shaped master bedroom.*

The north façade of the house was made to look more vertical by the addition of a two-story porch with its larger screened area cantilevered over the smaller entry porch below.

chilmark, martha's vineyard

OWNERS: John and Sharon DaSilva
ARCHITECTS: John R. and Sharon M. DaSilva, Polhemus Savery DaSilva Architects
PHOTOGRAPHER: Peter Mauss/ESTO

Fulling Mill Brook is at the bottom of a slope on five wooded acres in rural, "up island" Martha's Vineyard. It is an area of rolling hills and farmland, vigorous, tall trees, dirt roads, and brooks as fresh as mountain streams running next to old stone walls. The owners managed to find this picturesque piece of woodland, which had been overlooked by others due to strict building regulations. These were wetland regulations that prohibited construction in all but a tiny strip in one corner of the five

and a half acres. After one year of permit seeking and approvals, the owners were allowed to build a compact, 950-square-foot house on a tiny corner of the most expensive real estate in Massachusetts.

The proximity of large trees to the cottage influenced the owners to design with an architectural character reminiscent of a tree house. The north-facing entry facade was created with a gable shape, utilizing the full vertical height and vertical board-and-batten siding. The addi-

tion of a two-story porch with a large screened section on the second level, cantilevered side to side over a smaller entry porch below, accentuates the vertical illusion. The inspiration came from Victorian cottages and Gothic porches. The elevated porch is visible through a "cathedral" of green leaves when the house is approached from the main entrance. Its vertical nature pays homage to the quiet stature of the surrounding trees. The house's curves and brackets recall

LEFT: *The inspiration for the Gothic porch came from Victorian cottages, and a cathedral of trees.* RIGHT: *A simple, cost-efficient footprint and roof shape were used. The main living space rises into the roof, taking maximum advantage of minimal volume. Putting the living room on the second floor creates a dramatic space.*

Victorian Gothic trimwork and become a type of "branch" to the design of the house.

The central interior living space rises into the roof, maximizing the volume allowed by the height limitation. Placed at a higher elevation, rather than on the first floor, the living area becomes the most dramatic space in the interior, with a closeness to the treetops, where the beauty of the site can be fully enjoyed during the day. Sleeping is relegated to the lower level.

There are no traditional amenities, such as grocery stores, restaurants, or movie houses, in the neighborhood. The house is convenient to beaches and nature preserves if ever the owners should choose to leave their own wetland habitat and the orchestral variations of migrating birds' songs.

OPPOSITE: *The dining area's close proximity to the treetops provides abundant natural light.* RIGHT: *The stair entry to a second-level living area. The hallway leads to a cantilevered porch.*

LEFT: *The second-floor ceiling rises to the full height of the roof to give generous volume to the living space.* RIGHT: *Wood floors, comfort, and natural light embraced by full-leafed trees creates an island of contentment.*

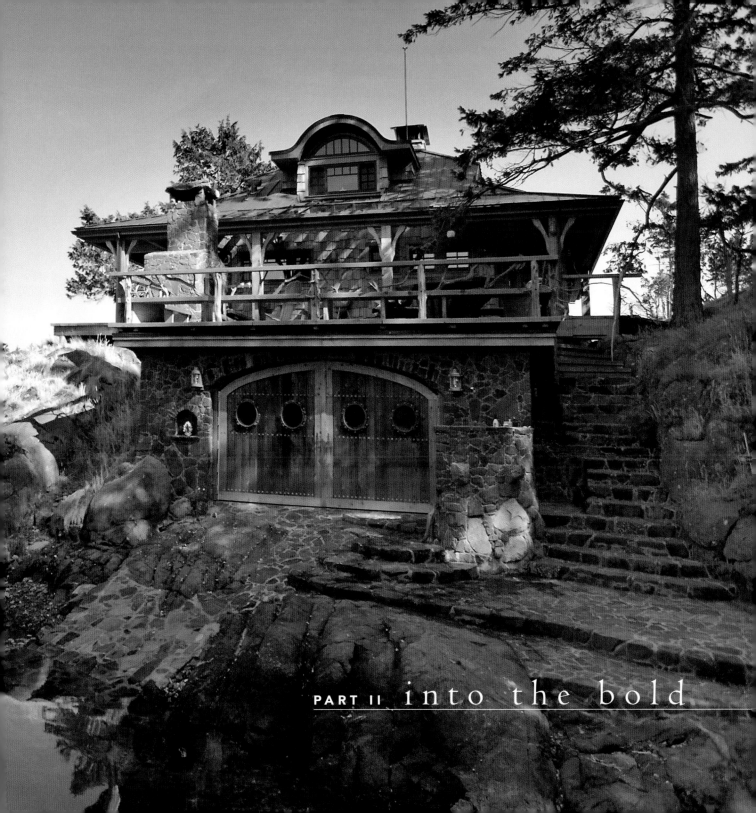

French doors of the main entry lead to the interior of the three buildings.

orcas island

OWNERS: Carol and Jonathan Buchter
ARCHITECT: David Coleman, David Coleman Architecture
PHOTOGRAPHER: Claudio Santini

The Buchters were living in Cleveland, Ohio, when they commissioned David Coleman to design their Orcas Island home. In today's fashion, the entire programming for the project, including initial meetings, was handled by telephone. The first time the Buchters met their architect was when they flew to Seattle to review the design proposal. They moved to Washington, where Carol is a cardiologist and Jonathan is the chief financial officer for the Seattle Monorail, a year after the house was finished.

This two-thousand-square-foot home is located in a fifteen-acre woodland, with large, charcoal-glacial boulders clad in thick, green moss; abstract scrub pine; and captivating madrona trees. The clients had long envisioned a cluster of buildings delicately scattered on their land. Staying within that vision, the architect created a modern rendition of the "summer camp" concept: sleeping pavilions, a central room for gatherings, and covered porches. The inspiration came from turn-of-the-century platform tents and national

park lodges. And in that vein, the design is a discriminating response to the light and heavy, the permanent and not-so-permanent natural features of the site. The composition, siting, and details of the house all reflect the unyielding quality of a natural ledge and the vulnerable nature of the adjacent pine forest.

A wide, timber-framed, enclosed glass porch spans sixty feet, providing the ordering element to the site and offering a connection for the three pavilions. The buildings are carefully placed atop the

The three separate structures are tucked in and out of the landscape. They are connected by a sixty-foot, glass-enclosed, timber-framed entrance porch.

glacial field to preserve the exceptional landscape. Each of the three buildings is positioned at an angle relative to the others and is oriented to certain views or unusual features in the landscape. Two of the pavilions are bedroom suites. The great room is in the third, with eleven-foot-wide barn doors that separate it from the porch. Interiors are finished with materials that again reflect the ruggedness and delicacy of the wildness outdoors. Airy cable lighting in the kitchen is offset by ground-face concrete block and ground-face concrete countertops. A warm and spacious interior literally brushes up against maple leaves that lean on the open windows. This house is perfectly in balance with its environment.

OPPOSITE: *A comfortable reading niche is tucked into the corner of the entrance hall.*
ABOVE: *The open and light entry is used as a gallery space.*

ABOVE: *The view from the kitchen table to the entrance hall on the left and into the living area on the right.* RIGHT: *The view from the opposite side of kitchen table, facing the area at the opposite end of the entrance hallway, which is a glassed-in sun room.*

OPPOSITE: *The living room shows strong architectural features combined with the light tilt-out, wood-framed windows. It can comfortably accommodate a group of twelve to fifteen.* ABOVE: *A bank of tilt-out windows surrounds the sun room at the end of the entrance hallway.*

LEFT: *The floor-to-ceiling two-sided Rumsford fireplace of ground-face concrete block and red brick marks the center of the room and soars into skylights, creating a balanced mass, light, and a volumetric composition.*

RIGHT: *Private bedroom suites are contained in two of the separate pavilions.*

An oasis is nestled into a grove of trees on ten acres of "high ground" on a 150-acre barrier island of salt marsh, in the Georgia low country.

eagle island

OWNER: Andy Hill

ARCHITECT: Tripp Alsbrook, Alsbrook Architects, Inc.

PHOTOGRAPHER: Richard Leo Johnson

Eagle Island is a barrier island among the backwaters and low country of the Georgia coast. One hundred and fifty acres of salt marsh and semitropical vegetation is crowned with ten acres of high ground and the added pleasure of pine and Georgia hardwood trees. The topography and vegetation offer an "island" of trees surrounded by marsh grass, and an island of marsh grass surrounded by waterways. The island is the habitat of eagles, and seventeen of their nests are visible from the porch of Andy Hill's retreat. The island has the tremendous advantage of deep-water access during all tides, making hopping from island to island—for exploring, fishing, or shrimping— as easy as a trip to the end of the dock and a leap onto the deck of a waiting boat.

This coastal marshland is a source of serenity and passion for Andy. His love of the inland waterways and the marshland habitat was a driving force in his pursuit of a sea captain's license. For the past fifteen years, Captain Hill has investigated the elaborate web of inland waterways and islands that flow into Doboy Sound in the Atlantic. By boat and in the air, he explores and maps islands, tiny harbors, canals, and secondary river systems.

The Eagle Island house took two years to build; all materials, of course, came in by boat. It is, foremost, an experience in solitude and privacy. The cottage is raised on posts supporting a large and unequaled screened porch that wraps entirely around the cottage and increases its square footage by another nearly fifty percent of livable space. The screened area is where the hot tub is installed, next

to the outdoor fireplace and an eagle observatory. Swings and "landscaping" make this area the most favored in the cottage. There is a large central room with a fireplace and game tables inside. Two bedrooms clad in cypress paneling are upstairs, and a tiny writing loft overlooks the activity below. The cottage was a collaboration between the owner and his childhood friend, architect Tripp Alsbrook. Tripp states that the island has everything the owner required, and the cottage they created is a celebration of the island's uniqueness. The crushed-shell walk from the dock makes getting to the boats very easy, yet it preserves Andy's need for isolated comfort.

ABOVE: *A heron leaves her post at sunrise.*
RIGHT: *The front entrance shows the elevated structure and spacious wraparound screened porch.*

OPPOSITE: *The porch with a view over the marsh to the water.* ABOVE: *The porch with a dining area and a view inland.*

ABOVE: *High ceilings in the wood-paneled bedroom.* RIGHT: *The writing loft above the living area.*

Joyce's painting studio, a short distance down the beach from the main house. The studio is twenty-by-twenty-feet square, with the north face of the roof made of glass. It sits on its own exquisite point of rock overlooking the bay.

deer isle

OWNERS: Gary and Joyce Wenglowski
ARCHITECTS: Peter Forbes, FAIA
PHOTOGRAPHERS: Paul Ferrino and Timothy Hursley

The unhurried drive to a local general store, post office, and specialty shop is a ten-mile glimpse of life on Deer Isle. Chosen by the Wenglowskis for its fragile beauty after a long and extensive search along the coast of Maine, the island offers seclusion without isolation. This is where the owners would enjoy their quiet contemplative avocations: Gary reads, Joyce paints, and both are avidly interested in the natural surroundings of this environment.

The summer of 2005 marks the twentieth anniversary of the design and completion of the project. Built in 1985, the house is set in a serene clearing bordered on its perimeter by birch and spruce forests, a rocky promontory, and the ocean itself. The "main" house is composed of two pavilions: one the master bedroom; the other, the living, dining, and kitchen areas. Each has concrete piers at the walls that support tubular trusses. Exterior walls, free of load-bearing functions, are made of glass. There is also the children's house, built when the children were young, and Joyce's painting studio. Together the family of small buildings is subordinate to the glass house, which serves as the parents' dwelling and the principal gathering place for meals and social activities. Standing free of the pavilion structures at each end are massive granite chimneys, with granite walls that extend under sloped roofs to form deep inglenook spaces by the fireplaces.

The house was never preconceived as a group of pavilions. It started to divide "like an amoeba" when it became apparent that the living, kitchen, and dining area with the great fireplace would become the spot where Gary could read, smoke his pipe, and contemplate his surroundings. The master bedroom became a further retreat for privacy, completely separate from the communal living space. Joyce's painting

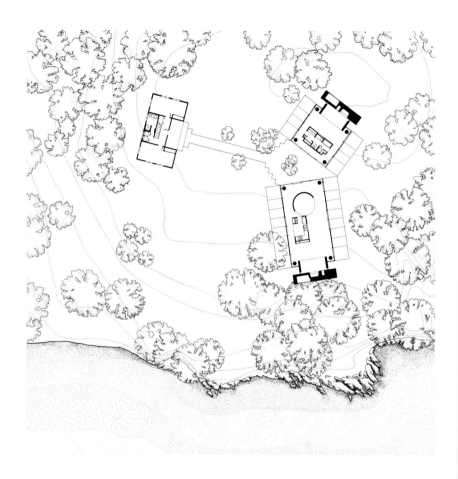

ABOVE: *A site diagram of the three main pavilions.* RIGHT: *The two main glass pavilions face one another and are bookended by their massive native stone fireplace walls.*

studio, sited on a gently curving, gray-green pebbled beach about a quarter of a mile away, is within the same family of shapes as the dwellings. The studio, however, had requirements of particular importance to an active, practicing painter: abundant north light, working surfaces inside, and outside space for painting and drawing.

LEFT: *Viewed from the rocky beach, the glass reflects the changes in the seasons.* ABOVE: *The pavilions are sited among the thin trees. In cloud shadows and an ever-changing sky, they are sometimes concealed.*

The children were teenagers when their house was built. Their idea of a vacation then significantly differed from their parents'. The daughter liked to be with a group of friends, listening to music (loud), eating pizza, and talking. The son played the electric guitar. Their pavilion had solid, soundproof walls, decks that opened to the forests for hanging out, its own laundry, bunk rooms, a kitchenette, and a loft.

Today, the family continues to use the house much as it was originally designed. Gary is now retired, but his reading has not diminished. Joyce now paints professionally, since the children have grown up. The children, now young parents themselves, use their former hangout as a guest house that can accommodate babies and their schedules equally well as the lives of rebellious youth.

Loons, weather, dawns, and sunsets are as constant as the sound of the ocean on the pebble beach. The house, too, is a constant, independent of time and the changes in the lives of its occupants.

ABOVE AND RIGHT: *The kitchen is its own separate enclosure in the larger volume of the living and dining pavilion.*

ABOVE: *The chimneys penetrate the structure walls, creating a large stone inglenook; almost a separate room.* LEFT: *The master bedroom pavilion houses another strong hearth using the chimney side as an interior wall.*

The cottage rests on its foundation of solid rock and the structure of the stone-walled boathouse below.

gulf islands

OWNERS: Charles and Theresa Walters
ARCHITECTS: Phil Kallsen, Kallsen Strouse Ishihara Architecture & Planning, Seattle, WA
PHOTOGRAPHERS: Michael Mathers, Charlie Walters

A dream began for Charlie Walters when he and his wife, T, sailed where the wind took them, fished, explored, swam, anchored, lived the good life, and began to dream. In his island manuscript, Charlie writes, "One island . . . charmed us, with its hand-hewn float house and intimate sheltered coves . . . we never knew its name, and could not forget its charm."

Lives, fantasies, disappointments, and resurrections intervened, but with a whim of steel and a few lucky breaks, Charlie managed to snare that same seductive island whose destiny it was to insinuate itself into their lives. Fifteen years

after the last time they had seen the island and a full year after they'd bought it, they arrived at its shore.

From Charlie's manuscript:
I stood in our boat and let my eyes roam over the rocky shores, in and out of the woods above them, and into the clear depths around us . . . as the water and trees cleared my thinking, in a manner that only wild things can do . . . our small island took hold of us. I had lived on the waters of Puget Sound most of my life, but now I saw how tame the south sound was. I had spent my time with friends who skied and wind surfed and climbed mountains.

Now their daring seemed strangely civilized, as I wondered what type of folks we'd find living in this remote place.

Charlie, Theresa, and their three boys stayed in the old float house on the island during their summers. The twenty-five-year-old float house was used as a guest house and home for the caretaker, and was moored in the intimate cove behind the cottage. The lumber and shakes were split out of logs washed up on local beaches, then either rowed or sailed home. New decking was built from yellow cedar that also washed up on local beaches. The float house was all handbuilt—no power tools (or power) were available on the island. The privy has one of the world's best views through the upper half of its Dutch door. Skylights in the roof keep it nice and bright inside. The wave in the roof mimics the curve of the water surrounding the island.

The Walters family learned about the ruggedness of this wilder place, especially about the unpredictabililty of the massive body of water around them that sets down its own rules and can very quickly accelerate foul weather and dangerous seas. Charlie and his friend, Phil, now an accomplished architect living in Seattle, began to design the island cottage. Plans were meticulous; the structure would be off the grid and sturdy.

The house was built using solar power with a generator to back it up. All water for the cement came from rain. The work crew commuted to the island daily in canoes, kayaks, and the odd motorboat from nearby islands. The materials were all barged in and winched up to the site on a farm cart over a temporary wooden plank roadway that was built over the shoreline rock. Their efforts disturbed as little natural landscape as possible, and as a result, wildflowers still bloom right up to the edge of the decks. The house was nestled down into the rocks to

The large barbecue fireplace and deck host summer gatherings and parties. Diners can be seated at a round table for fourteen at the opposite side of the deck.

make it as unobtrusive as possible.

Charlie and Theresa were very active in the design. They researched, explored, and selected every detail that complemented the overall design of the cottage. They learned to understand the working of every piece of equipment brought onto the island. Living on an island is an operation of concentrating on details; none can be overlooked. Planning is meticulous; supplies are sorted, weighed, packed, and stored to the maximum of efficiency. Every effort is ultimately for the greater good; individuals, neighbors, and strangers are all beneficiaries. A note from Charlie offers a glimpse of island life:

Note the copper roof, with down-spouts leading to a cistern and pump under the house. It pumps rainwater to cisterns on top of the island. Elevation distance gives us water pressure for water serving the house. All our water is caught on our roof. We have 12,000 gallons of storage; plenty as long as we are thrifty.

The view of the cottage from the lagoon in the rear shows the back deck, the boathouse below it, and the old float house, now used for visitors. The boathouse was built in a natural formation in the rock; its walls are made of rock collected on the island. Two large curved-top boathouse doors were built by a neighbor. Large portholes were salvaged from a sunken tug—some still decorated with their underwater remnants, their barnacles. Door handles are marine cleats; lights to the sides of the doors are old marine lanterns. To the right of the boathouse doors is the outdoor shower with shoulder-high rock stacked for a privacy wall in the front. This is the main area for outdoor activities: the gathering of friends who paddle over for the day's catch of shrimp, salmon, or clams; picking blueberries, wild salad greens, or apples for the rare apple pie.

There is so much to learn from Charlie and T, and the people they've found "living in this remote place." When Charlie's book, *Island Dreams*, comes out, get a copy and kick back in the hammock with it.

LEFT: *Splashes of color energize the interior of natural woods. Arched French doors off the kitchen let in natural light.*
RIGHT: *A beautifully hand-hewn stone and wood fireplace in the master bedroom with a ceramic jumping salmon surround.*
BELOW: *Dining in the glass-enclosed bay offers views of the surrounding lagoon and gulf.*

The large north-facing summer structure with decks and a portion of the 125-foot weather-viewing platform visible.

cape breton island

OWNERS: Bill and Esther Danielson
PROJECT TEAM: Brian MacKay-Lyons, Bruno Weber, Trevor Davies, Darryl Jonas, Brian MacKay-Lyons Architecture
PHOTOGRAPHERS: David Duncan Livingston, Bill and Esther Danielson

Northern exposure in Nova Scotia dramatically alters the way of living from summer to winter. This Cape Breton Island house changes its views and spatial arrangements to accommodate the seasons. In summer, it is essentially a large, north-facing (that is, ocean-facing) structure. The glass-enclosed sides of the house—three of them—expand the spaciousness and proffer panoramic views. Located on an isolated cliff edge on the tip of the island, the house has views across to Aspy Bay, to Cape North,

to the North Star, and, on a very clear summer day, to Newfoundland.

When winter arrives the house is modified to stand against the frigid weather and winds that blow up the cliff from the chunks of ice in the ocean below. Inside, the Danielsons rearrange their living habits to use a smaller, primarily south-facing space that lies inside the larger form. A large door/wall is rolled to close off the winter section of the house from the all-glass, north-facing summer design. A

canvas "ceiling" is lowered into place, reducing the large volumes of space in the high ceilings to create a cozier, warmer interior. One half of the big north side of the house is available for use during the winter months; however, the main living space is a protective environment within the heated core.

In Canada, there is a long tradition of treating buildings with the same highly admired craftsmanship and care used by boat builders. And, if properly maintained, the

Weather permitting, the entire house can open up to dissolve the boundaries between inside and outside. Views face across to Aspy Bay.

craft will last forever. Construction should be lightweight and mobile, whether on land, ice, or water. To take advantage of the economies drafted into this design the project was, to a large extent, prefabricated offsite with onsite assembly. The finger-jointed wood trusses sit on the flanking service boxes in a primitive "lean-to." Steel-clad, vertical sliding barn doors are recessed, like "eyelids," within the exterior envelope, providing a living weather skin. A 125-foot weather-viewing platform hovers above the ground parallel to the ocean. The owners, a meteorologist and a landscape architect, had specific design requirements for the architect to meet. Whether they are weather watching in the summer or snowshoeing in the winter, this house is ready for every season.

OPPOSITE: *The interior volumes are opened and expanded in the summer months by the stick-built trusses. To the left is a fireplace in the center of a wall of glass.*

LEFT: *The opposite view of the interior living area facing the fireplace and a reading cubby hole.* BELOW: *The interior dining area and reading cubby near the fireplace.*

The two connected "bunkies" of the cottage guest house. A screened porch allows guests to enjoy the island's unspoiled habitat.

spring island

ARCHITECT: Historical Concepts
DESIGN TEAM: Jim Strickland, Marty Mullin, and Shaun Yurcaba
PHOTOGRAPHER: Richard Leo Johnson / Atlantic Archives, Inc.

The owners of this house are New England residents who fell in love with the mild South Carolina climate and the natural beauty of Spring Island. Located between Hilton Head and the historic town of Beaufort, South Carolina, the island is in the heart of Carolina Low Country. The natural and rural character of the island's three thousand acres has been anchored in its ancient setting with the dedication of one third as a nature preserve. The island is home to hickory and live oak forests, wild

turkey, fox squirrels, deer, quail, and many varieties of wildlife.

The owners purchased a two-and-a-quarter-acre parcel, envisioning a true Southern retreat, and began planning Bee Tree Cottage. Located down one of the island's dirt roads, a gravel path meanders through the natural setting. The cottage is the guest house on their Bee Tree site. Two majestic oaks, beribboned with old Spanish moss and as beautiful as the old South herself, stood where the proposed cottage had been

planned to be built. The design team and the owners came up with an innovative alternative to the original plan. The cottage would integrate the oak trees by breaking the design, essentially, in two. Two sides of the cottage, now called the "bunkies," are connected to form an H, and the two-bedroom cottage is tucked under the existing tree canopy.

The clapboard siding and metal room of the cottage reflects the South's architectural heritage

The two-bedroom cottage is woven within the existing tree canopy. Live oaks, laden with Spanish moss blend into the H-shaped floorplan.

and the historic Low Country vernacular style. Each "bunkie" houses a private bedroom and a bath. Bead-board ceilings, heart pine floors, and horizontal cypress wall paneling add to the coziness and warmth of the bunkie. A soft, muted color palette of casual elegance and openness makes this 915-square-foot getaway a perfect "home base" for island living.

A narrow morning kitchen serves as a charming yet functional connector between the two bunkies. Situated between the two bedrooms, this arrangement allows privacy. In addition, a screened porch and a small sitting room allow space to enjoy indoor activities such as reading, conversation, and meditation amid the sounds of migrating birds in the nearby marsh grass and trees. The sights and sounds of this unique island setting can be fully experienced in this modest and unpretentious cottage, which blends perfectly into the island's simple and undisturbed heritage.

OPPOSITE: *A bunkie bedroom interior with open beams has plenty of space for guests.*

LEFT: *The bright morning-kitchen is in the central part of the cottage—the "pass-through" in the H design.* RIGHT: *A sitting area offers comfort and spaciousness, with just a hint of Caribbean warmth in the interior.*

PART III sailing into architecture

The outdoor exposure of the Rumsford fireplace made of concrete and steel.

vashon island

OWNERS: Colette and Kelly Quackenbush
ARCHITECT: Rex Hohlbein Architects
PHOTOGRAPHERS: Mike Jensen; Rex Holbein

Colette grew up spending her summers on Vashon Island in southern Puget Sound. To the northwest, just thirty-five miles by water, is Seattle. A mile or so from the southern shore of Vashon, a lush green piece of land cuts out into the Sound, appropriately named Point Defiance. In spite of its close proximity to large metropolitan areas, Vashon Island has maintained its purity and its mystery. Colette's family's Vashon summer house of the mid-1970 years was designed by architect William Booth, and *Architectural Record* recognized it as the "*Record House of the Year.*"

Married now with four children of her own, Colette and her husband, Kelly, live in a more traditional house on the outskirts of Chicago. When it came time to discuss and design a second home, the couple sought to build on Vashon Island and create a home that would embrace the qualities that Colette treasured from her childhood on the island. Translating childhood memories into contemporary architecture is a delicate process. Kelly and Colette brought a wealth of ideas and were very involved with their architect. Bringing their young family "out west" each summer was

a change of environment supported by the architecture.

The design guideline for the project came from the fateful schoolteacher's question on the first day of school, "So children, what did you do this summer?" The design also involved making a contrast between the formality of the family's house and daily life in Chicago, and the differences expected to occur during the freedom of summer. The children wanted a camplike experience, and helped develop a bunkhouse room, rather than individual rooms, to achieve that experience. The bunkroom is on the second floor;

it can be divided into two rooms with a large sliding plywood door, which nestles between two built-in bunks. The separation leaves one room to the north and the other to the south. The two rooms share a large floor-to-ceiling window to the east, facing the morning sunrise. The divider allows for a boy/girl separation when the kids have friends over and enables different families to occupy the upstairs as separate guest rooms. When the door is pulled back it offers a large floor area for playing games and other activities. The floor area that was saved by reducing

The up-slope side of the house showing the garage on right and views to the beautiful blue Puget Sound.

individual bedroom spaces was used to create a children's art room.

The selection of materials included plywood, steel, and concrete as finish materials, rather than the traditional plaster, painted wood, and brick. These materials were used in a way that will enrich the house and its environment over time, and will help the house fit perfectly and comfortably into its region. The simpler, the better.

ABOVE: *The down-slope side of the house looking up over grasses to the front porch.*
RIGHT: *An airy living room opens to the front porch and views of the Sound.*

OPPOSITE: *The living room has a Rumsford concrete and steel fireplace.*

LEFT: *Warm-toned wood panels offer extra storage at the front door.* ABOVE: *The kitchen adjoins the living room, creating an unbroken flow of space and light through the interior.*

A traditional slope and form from the historical Nantucket whalers' cottages.

nantucket

OWNERS: Kate and Lyman Perry
ARCHITECT: Lyman Perry
PHOTOGRAPHER: Bruce Buck Photography: Kristin Weber

There is a world that consists of nautical ways. Sea captains—men and women who live with salt spray in their faces—discover these ways through a lifetime spent on ships and smaller watercraft. Whenever there is time to spend on land, living within a contained and space-saving cottage is part of carrying out their nautical ways. Often theirs are ways of economy that brew in the soul and manifest in a daily routine of efficient activities. A balance of expertise and prudence always determined success on an island such as Nantucket. Maritime adventure was the underpinning of life on early Nantucket.

It is easy to think that when sea captains and whaling men spent time on land, they would build large houses as an antidote to the confinement of ship's quarters on long voyages. But that was not always so. Seamen's homes often took the shape of small shelters: tidy, compact houses, timber-framed and rectangular. Posts, beams, and rafters were mortised and tenoned together to withstand the force of storms. Lyman Perry, a naval officer, educator, and well-known Philadelphia architect, whose career includes having designed many island homes on Nantucket and elsewhere, has faith in the compact design of his home, about which he writes, "the wind may be blowing 40 to 60 knots, but I am snug and secure and I AM NOT offshore in the tempest. I am on 'my ship at sea,' the island of Nantucket."

The Perry's "ship at sea," is a one-acre site rustling up against one hundred acres of protected landscape flowing toward and ending at the shoreline. As is the tradition of true islanders, fiscal economy was a driving force when the land was purchased in 1979. The house was designed by Lyman for spatial efficiency, and was even prefabricated to reduce the costs of having building materials transported to the island.

The large living area is clad in cedar shingles to blend into the simplicity of the surrounding landscape. The large living structure is connected by the deck to a studio.

Lyman intended to build the smallest house possible with comfort and low maintenance in the style of the island's old whaling houses.

The compact first floor houses the living and dining areas within a twenty-by-twelve-foot space, and an almost square ten-by-nine-foot-six-inch kitchen. The second floor of the main house is composed of an open staircase that leads to two bedrooms and a bath. A pergola-covered breezeway connects the main level of the house to a guest house that has a bath and a half loft. Minor spatial adjustments in the past twenty-five years have been creating comfort and utility amid the beauty of the views: the moors with the water and the town in the distance. Modesty, pride, and satisfaction mingle in the sea breezes as Lyman concludes, "the space and home feels appropriately efficient, small but functional and I am not, in nautical terms, "over-boated!"

OPPOSITE: *A love for the sea inspired the owner/architect to design the cottage "like an old wooden whaling ship where you can actually see the beams shouldering weight."*

LEFT: *Painted white interiors emphasize the heft of the posts and beams. The divided windows are particularly suited to Nantucket's style and protect against heavy winds.* ABOVE: *Casual comfort is found in a sunny corner.*

OPPOSITE: *The entry is filled with marine and nautical mementos.*

ABOVE LEFT: *The second-floor master bedroom is bright with light and warm with wood flooring and furniture. The fan-shaped window was custom designed to admit afternoon light and to add visual interest to the room.* ABOVE RIGHT: *Angular, useful niches are created by the large posts.*

A lanai off the central living area is tucked under a broad overhang. For relaxation or entertaining, a bar at the kitchen window is on the right; at center is a table for dining.

north shore

ARCHITECT: Jim Niess, Maui Architectural Group
DESIGN TEAM: Margaret J. B. Sutrov; Dan Graydon
PHOTOGRAPHER: David Watersun

This *plein-air* house is located in rural Maui on the windward slopes of the 10,023-foot volcano Haleakala. Lunar and soot-covered, Haleakala has experienced at least ten eruptions in the past one thousand years, providing views to the summit of Haleakala from the house that are supernatural and rugged: a scene that is scattered with "young" cinder cones. The nearest town, Pa'ia, and the world-renowned windsurfing Hoopipa Beach, revered by windsurfers from Europe, South America, and the West Coast, are not far away. In mid-winter, during the birthing season, whales can be seen with mist geysers spouting from their nostrils from the front porch.

The North Shore house sits amid thirty-one acres of extraordinary landscape. Designed in the Polynesian tradition, the house has been assigned a discrete "pod" for each individual activity in a family home, and "active" spaces are placed at a respectful distance from "passive" spaces. An asymmetry of shapes minimizes the perceived volume of the three central pods, and a kitchen in the fourth pod, with adjacent outdoor dining, helps blend the structures further into their landscape. Open walkways and covered bridges connect the pods and promote natural cooling throughout the interior and around the exterior of the house. The main entry is a bridge that begins outdoors and continues through the front door to the interior. Open interior spaces with few interior walls offer a plentiful exchange of light between the inside and the outside.

The pods are sited to take in the 180-degree views of the ocean from the great room, master suite, and guest areas. Natural, managed,

Hawaiian hardwood is found throughout the living and leisure areas, where it is used as columns and posts. Landscaping is sculpted along the approach and around each pod dwelling: fragrant tropical flowers, colorful flowering shrubs, cocoa palms, and other native plants. A pool is placed at the center of a private and lush landscape on the mountainside of the house and protected from stiff trade winds. This is an island getaway on a getaway island.

ABOVE: *The exterior of the great room (showing lanai at front center) is the central "pod" in the group of structures.*
RIGHT: *The pool area is reached by taking a roofed walkway from the main house through an enclosure of heavily landscaped and fragrant vegetation.*

OPPOSITE: *The interior of the great room is spacious, airy, and filled with light; a natural cooling and air circulation system is promoted by the pod design.*

ABOVE: *The dining room is part of the great room. The atmosphere is enhanced by the sounds of a lovely water pond that flows into the room from the outside entrance.*
BELOW: *The master bedroom facing the ocean and views.*

The continuous undulations of the structural skeleton move along the rugged shore.

galiano island

OWNERS: Barry and Sophie Greenwood
ARCHITECTS: Kim Smith, MAIBC; Bo Helliwell, MAIBC Helliwell + Smith Blue Sky Architecture
PHOTOGRAPHER: Mark Darley / ESTO

Affectionately called "Fishbones" by the architects, this Gulf Island house design has a central spine, rafters sprouting to the sides, and a curving form in the front wall that give it the look of a fish fossil. The design also took its cues from the weather-sculpted sandstone beach on which it stands. Set on a shallow strip of land on the northwest edge of one of the southern Gulf Islands of British Columbia, the house is bounded by the water of the Tricomali Channel to the southwest and dense forest to the northeast. The weather here is the

mildest and best weather in Canada, receiving much more sun than shines on Vancouver.

In 1986, Barry Greenwood read a magazine article featuring the Blue Sky Architecture firm. The article was saved in a design file for the house he eventually would build. Barry had been a student at the University of Vancouver and was familiar with the Gulf Islands before he spent twelve years working in Indonesia, where he met Sophie. Together they spent one summer looking at land on all of

the southern Canadian Gulf Islands before they found a site that matched their idea of perfection. They contacted the architectural firm they had been waiting to work with for so long. While the house was in the design and construction phase, Barry maintained active involvement in the project with regular visits from Indonesia to Canada.

Parallel to the shoreline, a single fourteen-inch-thick ridge beam acts as the datum for a continuously modulating structural skeleton of

nine-inch-thick rafters. The undulations of the roof on the seaside were determined by water views, reflected light, existing vegetation, and the availability of shade. On the forest side of the land, a continuous skylight provides cool and dappled forest light.

The house is all one story on a level site. The Greenwoods wanted three bedrooms: one for themselves and one for each of their sons. Raising a young family on the island, both Barry and Sophie are active in island life, particularly with school and community organizations. In Jakarta, they were familiar with the use of desalination plants for drinking water and incorporated a similar system into their Gulf Island house. Groceries are available on the island, and for major items, a forty-five-minute trip by ferry to Vancouver or Victoria is available. The Greenwoods' Blue Sky design is an abstraction of natural phenomena, and at the same time, a finely tuned instrument for living in close proximity to the natural forces.

OPPOSITE: *The dining area is tucked into a niche of glass, stone, wood, and views to the bay.*

RIGHT: *Large posts and beams—and lights from a lengthy skylight—give volume and strength to the interior.*

LEFT: *Strong or delicate Asian pieces transform the interior.* OPPOSITE: *A Shoji screen and low furnishings reflect the use of natural materials inside.*

Atop the island of Bequia, this stone terrace is a perfect site for dinner parties, picnics, or a reading getaway.

moonhole

ARCHITECT: Tom and Gladys Johnston, Founders of Moonhole
PHOTOGRAPHER: John DiMaio

The Grenadines are a tropical archipelago in the eastern Caribbean. Anchored in the south by the large island of Grenada, the leeward Grenadines form a shallow crescent to the northeast that includes Union Island, the Tobago Cays, Canouan, Mustique, and other, smaller islands, culminating with the largest island of the group, Bequia, at the northern tip. Bequia is the home of a unique group of dwellings that were first built in the 1960s, when an advertising executive named Tom Johnston convinced his wife, Gladys, that they could leave their professions and live a wonderful life on the island.

A high, rugged stone formation that rises from the water and arches over a natural cliffside path is called "Moonhole." Tom fell in love with Moonhole and bought twenty acres surrounding the formation. He thought he would clear a small area for picnicking—his plan was to carve and lay stone steps leading to a small patio. In no time, Gladys and Tom found themselves living amid Moonhole rocks. Partial bedrooms, floors, and even a kitchen area began to take shape. As the story goes, a rock fell from his beloved Moonhole arch onto his bed. Undaunted, he moved to another site and started a new house. Over time the stone arches and patios, terraces and walkways—rooms that were open to the air—began to expand and other dwellings evolved. Now there are almost twenty residences on the Moonhole

The coast of Bequia and the sea lie below the house and the terraces, visible on the right.

land, and though Tom passed away four years ago, his free spirit reigns.

Paul Buettner owns a Moonhole dwelling on the top of Bequia. His house is at the highest point on the island, and its roof-top stone garden has a 360-degree view. Reading the stones of Moonhole is equivalent to reading the cliff dwellings of the ancient Anasazi in the southwestern United States. Few places are more simple, or as sophisticated.

The compound of dwellings is environmentally predisposed: rainwater is collected in cisterns and solar energy is used to generate electricity. Propane is used for cooking. Air conditioning is a part of the design, using covered stone pathways and open-air windows. The native stone floors and walls are solar collectors, maintaining steady temperatures during the day and releasing heat throughout the night. Nothing could be more beautiful.

OPPOSITE: *The rising moon can often be seen through this hole in the rock formations, giving the location its name.* LEFT: *A covered stone path separates the dining room on the right and the master bedroom on the left.* UPPER RIGHT: *A stone path and stone bench lead through the forest.* LOWER RIGHT: *The simplicity and beauty of an idyll is complete.*

ABOVE: *Interiors are always cool and breezy. Benches covered in brightly colored cushions and a large table create an ever-ready party space.* **RIGHT:** *The opposite side of the level that is open to the sea is a dining room, with stone benches, a wood table, chairs, end tables, and tropical foliage.*

Not far from the top of the island is the Brewer house, built up from the shore. From the water up is the pool area; two levels above that is the living area. Above and on the right is the master suite, and up on the left is the guest suite.

bequia - brewer's moonhole

OWNERS: Charles and Cornelia Brewer
ARCHITECT: Collaborative
RESTORATION: Charles Brewer, Architect
PHOTOGRAPHER: John DiMaio

Charles and Cornelia Brewer, a brave-hearted couple in active retirement, purchased one of Tom Johnston's Moonhole dwellings five years ago. The house had been abandoned for some time during the past thirty years and was derelict when the Brewers decided to buy it and begin a courageous tropical enterprise. Charles, an architect, knew the sort of work the place required: subtracting and adding spaces, trying always to honor the spirit of Tom Johnston's work without replication. Many years of sun and surf had pounded the site until concrete beams were crumbling and

falling into the sea. Remnants of the original design, trees and natural rock still in place, had become a ruin.

Charles and Cornelia set to the restoration and renovation project. They started with the rebuilding of beams and roofs and began deciding where they would add new spaces. This was one of Johnston's more adventurous designs, rising from the water up into the sides of the rock cliff and into the hillside. Not to mention there were no straight lines in the "design" and the dwelling is open to the sea on every level. Charles managed to get

a generator to power a few tools to begin the project, as there is no electrical current at Moonhole.

The founder's basic convenants for Moonhole included the use of only indigenous island materials; all structures to be integrated into the site; a minimum disturbance of the land; no straight lines, nothing to destroy the natural ambiance; no engine noise, telephone poles, garish paint, or reflective surfaces. Originally no windows were allowed. Fresh water was to be collected from roofs and stored. When asked what to do when it

LEFT: *Lanterns light the way at dusk under the deliciously scented frangipani tree.*
RIGHT: *This extraordinary seawater pool combines the sea, a hidden beach, and a private island dream.*

and platform, and the sea wall. The details created by Charles and Cornelia are well-designed accents such as soft arches and small hardwood drawers and closets. Stonework in the master bedroom is as beautiful as Frank Lloyd Wright's recipe for "desert concrete." Every nook and niche is put to use. Benches and couches are built in.

At sea level is an extraordinary seawater swimming pool separated from the ocean by a wall of stone arches. The pool's organic shape feels as though it is a large tidal pool on the beach. A lookout area can be reached only by swimming across the pool. Other charming follies express the lively imaginations fired by the freedom of a team that lives on the edge. Below are white sand beaches against the tropical blue ocean. Eight miles off the terrace, the islands of Mustique and Petite Mustique are visible.

Charles and Cornelia love their grotto. Always looking for the chance to make a minor adjustment here or there, they enjoy the evolution of architecture in flux.

rained, Johnston replied "step back." Johnston supervised every inch of Moonhole's development and construction. He once told Charles that he had made only one mistake and that had been rectified by a bolt of lighting.

The intense renovation of 90 percent of the Ravine Landing dwelling included rebuilding terraces, guest rooms, the swimming pool

LEFT: *A living room is complete when its furnishings include a chess set, a couch in a grotto, and a whalebone coffee table.* ABOVE: *The open-air vanity in the guest bath has views to Mustique on the left and Petite Mustique on the right.* BELOW: *The master suite is designed for the comfort of a reinvigorating, cool night's sleep.*

PART IV *harmonizing mysteries*

The house is located on an eight-acre, high bank waterfront of granite cliffs and grasslands.

rainbow rock

OWNERS: Ginny Gilder and Lynn Slaughter
ARCHITECT: Balance Associates
DESIGN TEAM: Tom Lenchek, AIA; Scott LaBenz, AIA; Timothy Posey
PHOTOGRAPHER: Steve Keating Photography

This eight-acre site is on a high bank waterfront located on a small peninsula of Lopez Island in Puget Sound. Open grasslands share the site with granite boulders and wooded areas. Ancient Native American burial grounds cover portions of the eight acres. Prior to the design phase, the owners, architects, and preservation and conservation representatives met. Topographic surveys, archeological surveys, and documentation were made to eliminate the possibility of site disturbance and to find an appropriate building location.

The views and amenities of the site guided the design in concert with the many imposed restrictions.

The high, rocky bank is naturally terraced into two levels that are separated by a twenty-foot rock face. The house is located on the lower terrace, while the upper terrace was left untouched. The two terraces are connected by a bridge spanning the cliff and a stair tower, making it an easy getaway for the children to play in the upper field. The house was planned as a weekend retreat and a summer home by an active family

with plans to make it a permanent residence in the future. It is divided into three central areas: a guest area, a play wing for the children, and the main house with the owners' suite above on a separate floor. The guest house and the children's bunkhouse are connected to the main house via a glass-walled bridge, which doubles as a sitting room for reading and enjoying the views of the Sound. This part of the house can be closed off from the main house with a sliding door so the house does not feel large and empty when only the

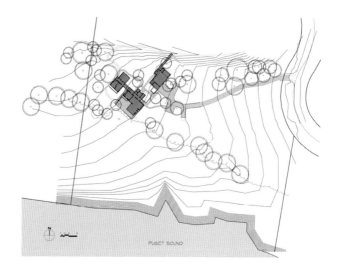

PUGET SOUND

RIGHT: *A lighted stair tower connects the barn playroom bridge to the upper play field.*

owners are there. Thus, the plan provides space for larger groups of friends for entertaining and still offers an intimate scale for a private getaway for two.

The barn functions as a kids' indoor play area with its sleeping loft, bathroom, heated workshop, and storage for bikes and boats. The loft area opens up to a view of the outdoor play field above a small rock bluff. A glazed stair tower leads to a bridge to the upper field.

Natural materials that reflect the setting are granite, cedar, and stucco, and run from the exterior of the house to the interior. A large outdoor terrace on the south side of the house is partially sheltered by a roof that becomes the cover for the living room. The living room is enclosed by three window walls and large sliding doors that lead to the outdoor terrace. In contrast, solid forms made of granite and wood give the sensation of enclosure and shelter. Black concrete floors run from the indoors out to the patios for a full interior and exterior exchange of experiences.

ABOVE: *The barn functions as the children's indoor playhouse, with a sleeping loft. A glazed glass stair tower opens up to a bridge that provides a path to the upper play field (on right).* RIGHT: *The house is composed of three areas: the lower living area; the second-floor master suite; and a children's bunkhouse and guest room connected by a glass walled bridge.*

OPPOSITE: *The living room has large sliding doors to the outside terrace. Black concrete floors flow from the indoors to the outdoors for a continuous visual connection.*

ABOVE: *The soft maple cabinetry and sleek lines of the kitchen complement the living room.* BELOW: *The second-level master bedroom suite has views to the water.*

The character of the house lies in its height and the wraparound windows that take advantage of the views.

aquinnah, martha's vineyard

OWNERS: Tony and Karen DaSilva
ARCHITECTS: John R. and Sharon M. DaSilva, Polhemus Savery DaSilva Architects Builders
PHOTOGRAPHERS: Peter Mauss / ESTO; Randi Baird

This stunning house is nestled into a portion of three level acres in a small valley, east of the Gay Head Lighthouse. The valley widens at both the South and the North, providing second- and third-floor views to the ocean in each direction. Partially open fields are bordered by old stone walls and wooded with small oaks that are continuously sculpted by the whirling winds.

The Gay Head Lighthouse and its perpendicularity dominate the context for this house. The property was originally thought to not have a water view, but the architects' review of the USGS contour map indicated that it should. After the climbing of a nearby tree, it was discovered there is indeed a water view, which improves as the elevation ascends. A compact, three-story house was designed to have an affinity with its landscape similar to the lighthouse. Both appear tall and vertical as they emerge from the scrub oaks that blanket the adjacent hills. The houses on this remote part of the island are spaced far from each other. Thematically they share white cedar shingle cladding, minimal exterior paint, and orientation to the view.

The house is situated on a line drawn through its center and out to the lighthouse. The tall space, limited to twenty-eight feet by zoning restrictions, and its central windows provide a view up to the treetops and to the lighthouse beyond. From the third-floor interior window, the lighthouse appears centered in the round exterior window that is across the clerestory level of the living room below: a reminder of what it meant to see the lighthouse from a porthole in a passing ship. It is an engaging scene: delicate, thought provoking and, ultimately, hypnotizing.

A cherished view of the Gay Head Lighthouse is the grounding feature for this otherwise isolated house.

The house is a compact 1,850 square feet and suited to this family of five for weekends, holidays, and summers. Four bedrooms and privacy for the adults were requisite within a minimum of square footage. Sunlight filling the interior was a high priority for owners. The main living level on the second floor has an open floor plan and a tall ceiling in the living room to make the small space feel bigger. Wraparound windows also expand the space and offer views in every direction. The space is filled with light at all times of the day.

The climbing tree is still there for the pleasure of the owners' three children and will always be a measure of the view.

OPPOSITE: *The compact footprint and the openness of the design are enhanced by the large outdoor porch on the second floor, and the porthole view of the lighthouse on the top floor.*

ABOVE: *Sunlight floods into the second-floor living and dining area.* RIGHT: *The upper-level bedroom emerges out of the second floor and has views of the ocean.*

This island house rises out of a rocky knoll above a lake and views of the neighboring San Juan Islands.

decatur

ARCHITECT: Michael Canatsey Associates
PHOTOGRAPHER: Chris Eden

The American San Juan Islands exist in a shimmering air and water world. The smell of the water itself is a sensory-revitalizing tonic found where the salt waters of the Pacific Ocean flow into the icy fresh waters from the bountiful mountain streams that surround and replenish Puget Sound. The siting of this house is remarkable for its views of the Sound and the added treasure of a fresh water lake below.

Designed for a family of four, the house has two stories. It sits on a rocky knoll oriented toward the neighboring islands to the north, the fresh water lake and woodlands to the south. There is no ferry service to the island; travel by private boat means careful planning for meals, recreation, and other needs. The owners bring bags and bags of groceries, books, games, and recreational gear with them up the dock from the boat landing.

The textured concrete exterior walls of the lower floor are colored to eventually blend with the natural rock outcroppings. Over time, moss and lichen will attach to the walls and create the impression that the structure grows out of the hillside above the beach below. The lower level houses a modest guest room, a bath, and the children's bunk room. At the upper level, a wall of large glass walls can slide open to the teak deck that wraps around the living spaces. The deck juts into the treetops and links the living room and dining areas to the fresh air and the voluptuous, peeling native madrona trees. A dramatic view of the quiet cove below is an added jewel.

The floor-to-ceiling precast concrete fireplace hearth has a nook for wood storage and a broad bench for sitting. Floors and countertops are made of tile and concrete. The grays of the concrete contrast with the warm stained wood beams, ceilings, window frames, and the outdoor decking, echoing the surrounding ruggedness. This is a home that requires low maintenance in favor of the pursuit of nature.

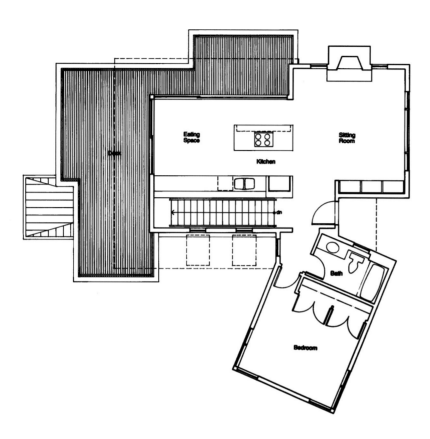

ABOVE: *The floor plan.* RIGHT: *The design and materials are intended to obscure the house and, over time, to allow it to blend into the surrounding landscape while also reflecting it.*

Eating Space

Sitting Room

Kitchen

Deck

dn

Bath

Bedroom

OPPOSITE: *The beautiful teak deck wraps around the living spaces and perforates the foliage for dramatic views of the quiet cove below.* ABOVE AND RIGHT: *The concrete floor-to-ceiling fireplace and precast hearth are flanked by windows to continue the views around the living room.*

A sheltered deck on the ocean side of the house is out of the wind and offers a good place for reading or dining.

great cranberry island

OWNERS: Rodman and Susan Ward
ARCHITECT: Peter Forbes, FAIA Architects
PHOTOGRAPHER: Timothy Hursley / The Arkansas Office

This location is a very special place on earth; in fact, it is quite extraordinary. Located on the southeast coast of Great Cranberry Island, the property extends from a dense spruce and birch forest down to an open meadow above a steep basalt ledge and the sea. The panorama of the ocean is unbroken. Two small, uninhabited islands are ten miles off to the south, but otherwise there is nothing but the vast sweep of the North Atlantic to the east and southeast. In fine weather the ocean to the south is a caldron of light: brilliant, dazzling, and often blinding. Cranberry, being one of the islands farthest from the coast, is, however, often shrouded in dense fog. Even while other westerly islands are sunny, there are days, even weeks, when visibility on Cranberry Island is less than fifty yards. Winter storms, not deflected by any other land, beat upon its shore; severe wind and sheets of water literally lash the site. The Wards wanted the house to be both a "porch" from which to enjoy the panorama and a refuge from the elements.

The house becomes a line drawn at the edge of the forest and facing the open meadow. On one side all is open and almost desolate in its exposure to the intense sun, wind, and salt. On the other side is the sheltering spruce forest, an intimate landscape of moss, ferns, and filtered green light. It is what the architect likes to think of as an "Eliot Porter landscape," where, in the photographs by the master of the Maine coast, a universe can be experienced in a square yard. The intense ocean side is too compelling to be ignored, but it can become overwhelming. The forest side is the soothing and restful antidote. And the house became a filter—open equally to both sides.

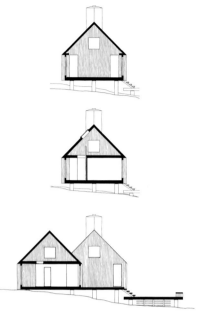

On a remote island, building is never easy. Every item of material must be brought by boat—weight and bulk kept to a minimum. Yet the environment of an island in the North Atlantic is harsh, and materials that are insubstantial quickly deteriorate. The construction of the Ward house was conceived of as a boat: materials impervious to a marine environment, such as teak, cedar, bronze, and copper, were selected. Stone was cut on shore to sizes that could be lifted by one man.

The Cranberry Island project began when the Ward family consisted of the parents and four children, the eldest married and the three younger ones still in school and college. An immediate requirement was to provide adequate yet sufficiently separate spaces so that the parents, kids, and friends could live in harmony. The son was an avid athlete, so the ultimate test was to accommodate his entire lacrosse team while the parents were home. The solution was distance. The parents' bedroom, sitting room, and private porch are at one end of the main pavilion, and the guest bedrooms, dormitory, and children's porch are at the other end. In between is a sequence of spaces alternating from private to public. The essence of the Ward house is its role as a vessel and a catalyst for vibrant family activity. Everything—site, ocean, and house—is a context for their family life. The family, in all its various transformations, loves the land, the views, the forest, and the sea, but they always return to their principal enjoyment: spending time together.

ABOVE: *Floors are made of Douglas fir, and ceilings are clad in cedar.* RIGHT: *The kitchen, dining room, and living room are spaced at sixteen-foot intervals. Each is defined by an opening that grows progressively wider as it recedes from the fireplace.*

ABOVE: *Large mahogany framed slider doors connect the bedrooms to the forested side of the house.* RIGHT: *Another bedroom features an attached deck and views of the endless horizon. There are no further islands beyond Great Cranberry Island.*

The rhythm of the windows introduces the large interior living space.

islesboro

ARCHITECT: Jeremiah Eck Architects
PHOTOGRAPHER: John DiMaio

A thirty-minute ferry ride away from Lincolnville, on the coast of Maine, is Islesboro Island. The island has a small year-round population and a much larger summer crowd. This family began as part of the summer crowd many years ago. The house now stands on property where the original summer cottage was built by the owner's grandfather, who started the Islesboro tradition of visiting in the summer. As a child, the owner spent his summers here. The island is small, and the summer residents are well known to the year-round residents. A few stores are scattered around for essentials. Having no real "downtown"

has helped to insure the historic charm of the island.

This cottage was built inexpensively by most standards. The exposed wood trusses—prefabricated trusses normally used in the attics of spec-built homes—are painted white and are delightfully intricate on the interior. The open-framed walls and a high, painted wood ceiling accompany the rhythm of the trusses with an airy cadence. A complement to the delicacy of the trusses and open framing are the cutout partitions that form a railing and banister on the stair, a wall and loft railing behind and above the stair, and a room partition in the

upper loft space that divides the large, open space into two semi-private sleeping areas.

The large first-floor living space is dominated by a floor-to-ridge-beam river rock fireplace, as well as a wall consisting of all windows. Natural light floods the living area, which is comfortably arranged for dining, reading, and kids' activities. A kitchen, mudroom, and bedroom complete the first floor. The total square footage of the entire cottage is a modest 1,600 square feet. The board-and-batten siding is reminiscent of grandfather's cottage days, and the family tradition carries on in his spirit.

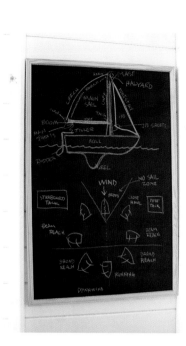

ABOVE: *The chalkboard presents an important nautical lesson for everyone.* RIGHT: *The porch at the front door is convenient for use as a casual dining area attached to the screened-in room.*

OPPOSITE: *The one large area on the main level consists of a large living space, a kitchen, one bedroom, and the mudroom. The floor-to-ceiling windows and fireplace create a sense of exuberance.*

ABOVE: *An open stair leads to the kids' loft space above.* RIGHT: *The loft is separated into two areas for the children.*

Architect Roland Terry's keen sense of style and use of salvaged materials resulted in a modern vernacular form for this site.

san juan islands

ARCHITECT: Roland Terry

PHOTOGRAPHER: Dick Busher

The idea of a dwelling being "true" island architecture, that is, an aboriginal creation, is seldom considered, if considered at all. Roland Terry's island masterpiece is an artifact of human effort that pulsates with the roar of Puget Sound; of human gifts and those of nature. The simple dwelling, built upon its perfectly chosen roost, is strengthened by the symbolism of the previous century of Pacific Northwest coastal culture. A certain evolution of neo-modernism can be seen in the house and its interiors. Vestiges of urban cultural artifacts from French, African, and

Asian countries, circa 1950, were meant to flow into the setting.

A house with a sod roof might evoke the work of Alvar Aalto: similar in scale, materials, and climate. Like Aalto, Terry adapted outdoor materials for structural and exposed use on the interior. Very large structural posts—old-growth timbers turned to driftwood—were found on surrounding beaches. Seventeen of the oversized posts were salvaged for the construction of the house and appear at exterior and interior corners. On the interior, the massive posts divide large expanses of floor-

to-ceiling, rolling-window walls; they are also used as elemental columns near hallways and doorways. Stripped of bark and cleaned, the timber posts appear as ancient as the stone columns in Rome. One hundred years before Terry built his island dwelling, the First Nation Haida priest, Chief Weah, built a winter retreat utilizing tall timbers. The vertical wood planks found on the exterior of his large, long house inspired those used in Terry's island house. Ironically, Chief Weah had imported English chairs, similar to those used by Terry in his dining

ABOVE: *The lawn between the two buildings, where no trees were cut, is a good place for a badminton game on a windless day, or for getting a little sun.* OPPOSITE: *An outdoor terrace is complete with a fire pit and a mosaic pattern that flows throughout the grounds.*

room. Each had salvaged many other usable objects from the beaches, in the tradition of "cargo-cults."

Terry's furnishings and decorative accents were gathered from villages and cities worldwide. His floor and patio, however, are made of concrete and stones, displaying a mural of waves that flow from the outer terraces to the interior rooms and throughout hallways. Every wall, window, and door he installed opens in the way of French doors and windows or Dutch doors. As the building aged and gained its silvery patina, its handsome profile became as much a part of the landscape as the windblown trees. He had moved his original building site so as not to disturb the trees; he modified the shape of the house; and he adjusted his own expectations. Terry's reverential treatment of the land and the region keeps the water and tree spirits alive and happy on his island.

LEFT: *The library and dining room are connected by the flowing mosaic and the large salvaged driftwood posts.*
ABOVE: *The open and elegant living room is accentuated by several of the large peeled logs that Terry used throughout the house.*

ABOVE AND RIGHT: *Stone walls, open beam ceilings, and five enormous posts evoke a Haida Indian long house. The glass set between the large posts adds a touch of modernism to the design, and an overall new vernacular has been created.*

PART V recycling the universe

Lava fields are home to new growth over time. Life is beginning to emerge from both nature and man after the 1955 eruption of the volcano at Kilauea.

lava flow

OWNER: Robert Trickey
ARCHITECT: Craig Steely, Architect
PHOTOGRAPHER: JD Peterson; JD Peterson Photography

Designer Robert Trickey first saw the "intense otherworldly beauty" of the lava flow landscape and decided to build his contemporary modernist house on the rocks. The site is located near Kilauea caldera on the eastern side of Hawaii's Big Island. Down slope from the ridge called the East Rift Zone, a large crack caused by and connected to the volcano's movements runs from the crater to the west, all the way to the deep sea in the far northeast. Lava can travel sideways through the crack and escape at any weak spot on its way toward the ocean. The lava flow on

which Robert's house is built occurred in 1955, an enormous event that escaped the rift zone in five locations. A similar occurance could happen tomorrow, or perhaps in 150 years.

There are no zoning regulations preventing construction from taking place on the lava flow. The site borders an eight-mile section of the flow that is state-owned and will never be developed, so his privacy is assured. He is in love with the lavascape, especially with the white stuff that grows on the lava and looks like snow, but is actually called lichen (or *Limu-o-Pele*, which means

Pele's algae or Pele's snow, Pele being the goddess of the volcano).

Robert's concept was to have the house frame the lava field. Craig designed it so that upon arrival, visitors see the house visually float above the lava field. One climbs a concrete stair onto a plateau of cut lava rock. From this vantage point the house is visible sitting behind a pool, framing the lava and sky with structure and line. From there a bridge crosses the pool to the lanai.

The design of the house is essentially two boxes. The lower, more transparent box is the space that

ABOVE: *The view is otherworldly in the landscape outside Robert's bedroom.* RIGHT: *At the center of a field of lava, the sense of adventure and composure permeate the house.*

houses the lanai and living rooms, kitchen, dining, and guest room.

The upper box is the master suite, which is a long tube with glass at each end. The east-end windows have views of the sunrise and the lava flow; the west end views the plume of steam where the hot flow enters the ocean, the sunset, and, at night, the startling view of the hot red and white lava reflected from the bottom of the clouds above the caldera, back down to the earth.

Robert reserved much of the design work for himself and his own time frame. He designed the interior furniture and lighting plans. His work also includes the built-in case goods such as the mango and steel interior staircase. Robert selected all the finish details and the materials. The project is the result of the innovative collaboration between owner and architect.

Fifty years have passed since the lava flow emerged. Robert watches over Pele's snow as it turns into soil. He waits for tiny fern starts to take hold. Soon ohia trees, sacred to Pele, will get their footing, clinging to the lava rocks with their tiny hairlike roots. Robert notes the multitudes of insects, birds, lizards, mice, and every evolutionary creature that makes its home in the crevices of stone. Robert named his new home *Pohakunani,* "the Beautiful Rocks."

LEFT: *The house and a studio are separated by a large lanai. At night, from the lanai, the red glow of Kilauea crater is visible and is reflected by the underbody of low hanging clouds.* ABOVE: *The lower, more transparent form contains the lanai, living room, kitchen, dining room, and a guest room. It is clad in black glass, which reflects the lava.* BELOW: *Just outside the living room is a compact lanai, perfect for a swimmer's launch into the pool.*